Paranormal Field Guides

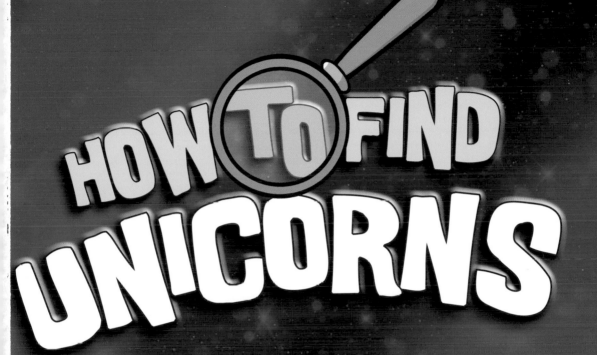

HOW TO FIND UNICORNS

Thomas Kingsley Troupe

BLACK RABBIT BOOKS

Hi Jinx is published by Black Rabbit Books
P.O. Box 227, Mankato, Minnesota, 56002.
www.blackrabbitbooks.com
Copyright © 2023 Black Rabbit Books

Marysa Storm, editor; Michael Sellner, designer
and photo researcher

Library of Congress Cataloging-in-Publication Data
Names: Troupe, Thomas Kingsley, author.
Title: How to find unicorns / by Thomas Kingsley Troupe.
Description: Mankato, Minnesota : Black Rabbit Book, 2023. |
Series: Hi Jinx. Paranormal field guides | Includes bibliographical
references and index. | Audience: Ages 8-12 | Audience: Grades 4-6 |
Summary: "With fun facts, a colorful design, and critical thinking
questions, How to Find Unicorns inspires readers to take their love of
the paranormal to the next level all while laughing and learning"–
Provided by publisher.
Identifiers: LCCN 2020034526 | ISBN 9781623107208 (hardcover) |
ISBN 9781644665695 (paperback) | ISBN 9781623107260 (ebook)
Subjects: LCSH: Unicorns–Juvenile literature. | Animals, Mythical–
Juvenile literature.
Classification: LCC GR830.U6 T76 2022 | DDC 398.24/54–dc23
LC record available at https://lccn.loc.gov/2020034526

Image Credits

Shutterstock: Aleksandr Bryliaev, 14, 17; Aluna1, 13, 18;
Antracit, 8–9, 20; Arcady, 12; ArtHeart, 6; ayelet-keshet,
6–7; benchart, 6–7; Christopher Hall, 15; Christos
Georghiou, Cover, 13, 18; DEYASA_346, 10, 11; dibrova,
14; DM7, 2–3, 14; Dualororua, 15; ekler, 8; Frederick
R. Matzen, 2, 3; Galyna G, 3, 4, 7, 8, 9, 13, 16, 17, 18;
gigello, 14; hanibacom, Cover, 1, 5, 9, 21; HitToon,
Cover, 1; imaginasty, 14; Memo Angeles, Cover, 5, 7,
13, 16, 18, 21; monbibi, 5, 14, 17; My Life Graphic, 5,
16–17; Nearbirds, 16–17; Pasko Maksim, 11, 19, 23, 24;
Pitju, 4, 17, 21; Ron Dale, 3, 4, 8, 15, 20; totallypic, 5,
14; TRONIN ANDREI, 18; ViMin, 4, 5, 16, 17, 22, 23

CONTENTS

Chapter 1
ON THE HUNT

Did I hear it right? You want to find unicorns? Then you've come to the right place. I've been tracking unicorns since I was three. When it comes to these horned horses, I'm the best. So is this guide. It's your ticket to unicorn nation!

Thomas Kingsley Troupe

Thomas Kingsley Troupe isn't well-known for his unicorn research. But he sure loves writing about them. He claims to have seen hundreds of unicorns. We asked him for proof. He said he had some, but his dragon burned it. We then asked to see the dragon. He said it flew away.

5

Handy and Helpful

It's hard to believe, but you're only a few pages away from success. This handy guide will make your dreams come true. You'll learn gobs of galloping unicorn facts. In no time, you'll know where they live and what they eat!

A unicorn's horn is called an alicorn.

So saddle up! And keep this book close on your unicorn quest. It'll be like having me running across rainbows with you. Just remember not to look down.

Chapter 2

CREATURE CHARACTERISTICS

You probably know unicorns are horses with horns. But these horns have unique features. They're pointy, shiny, and often a bit twisty. Most unicorns are white. I've seen them in a few different colors, though. But if you spot a **beige** one, it's a fake. Unicorns are never beige.*

*Expert's Note

Don't be fooled by fake unicorns. Some horses put ice cream cones on their heads. They're trying to trick people into giving them attention.

Behaviors

Most experts think they know about these creatures. They say unicorns love happiness and sweet smells. Some think unicorns **purify** water with their horns.

But I've seen unicorns that didn't care about any of that. They're often **territorial**. They don't make friends easily. I even saw one shoot a laser from its horn. It melted a playground into a puddle of goo. No children were hurt, but the park was never the same.

Stories say unicorns live for hundreds of years.

Diet

Unicorns are pretty much horses, so they eat what horses eat. They **graze** on grass and flowers. They're not all plant eaters, though. Some unicorns out there want to eat people.* My friend Jeff and I ran into some angry unicorns. They took one look at us and ran after us like bloodthirsty broncos. We hid in a tree for two days until they left.

*Expert's Note
It's better to be safe than sorry. Wear bite-proof clothing when searching for unicorns.

Some people call narwhals
the unicorns of the sea. Their
tusks look like unicorn horns.

Chapter 3

WHERE TO FIND THEM

Unicorns are some of the hardest creatures to find. They like places where rainbows end and rabbits sing. These **enchanted** forests are hard to find, though. And even then, unicorns can be tough to spot. You're more likely to get a magical wood **tick**. *

Tracking the Creatures

You'd think tracking these fantastic foals would be easy. All you'd need to do is follow hoofprints, right? Wrong. Follow any ol' hoofprints, and you'll just find a horse. Because unicorns are magical, they leave a different kind of track.

In the middle of their prints, you'll see a special shape. It might be something like a flower or heart. The shape depends on their mood.*

*Expert's Note

Hoofprints with lightning bolts once led me to a unicorn. I named him Stormy.

Approaching the Creatures

If you've reached this page, I'm sure you've found a unicorn. But now what? Well, unicorns can be crabby. So just make sure to smile. And just keep calm. Maybe they'll let you take a selfie. Ask nicely, and they'll belch out a rainbow or two.

And yes, you can just send any thank you gifts directly to me. Because of this guide, you know how to find unicorns!

Scotland's national a
is the unicorn. For

Chapter 4

GET IN ON THE HI JINX

Unicorns aren't real. People love stories about them, though. In fact, unicorn tales go back hundreds of years. Visit your library to find these stories. Use the Internet to learn why people started telling them. The facts behind these magical animals might surprise you!

Take It One Step More

1. Stories say unicorn horns have different powers. What do you think the horn is used for?

2. Pretend you found a unicorn. Would you try to catch it or leave it alone?

3. Some people believe unicorns grant wishes. What would you wish for?

GLOSSARY

beige (BEYZH)—a color that is a light grayish-yellowish brown

claim (KLAYM)—to say something is true when some people might say it's not true

enchanted (en-CHANT-uhd)—having or seeming to have a magical quality

graze (GRAYZ)—to feed on growing plants

purify (PYOOR-uh-fahy)—to make pure

territorial (ter-i-TAWR-ee-uhl)—trying to keep others away from an area that someone or something uses or controls

tick (TIK)—a tiny animal with eight legs that is related to the spider and attaches itself to humans and animals from which it sucks blood

LEARN MORE

BOOKS

Braun, Eric. *Taking Care of Your Unicorn.* Caring for Your Magical Pets. Mankato, MN: Black Rabbit Books, 2020.

Clarke, Ginjer L. *Are Unicorns Real?* Penguin Young Readers. New York: Penguin Young Readers, 2021.

Owings, Lisa. *Unicorns.* Mythical Creatures. Minneapolis: Bellwether Media, Inc., 2021.

WEBSITES

Totally Crazy Monster Myths (That Are Actually True)
kids.nationalgeographic.com/explore/monster-myths/

Unicorn Facts
www.softschools.com/facts/fiction/unicorn_facts/2517/

Unicorn - Kids
kids.britannica.com/kids/article/unicorn/390060

INDEX